A-LEVEL CH

FLASH NOTES

OCR B YEAR 2

New Syllabus 2015

Dr C. Boes

Condensed Revision Notes (Flashcards) for Successful Exam Preparation

Designed to Facilitate Memorization

For corrections, comments and special offers go to:
www.alevelchemistryrevision.co.uk

Text copyright © 2015 Dr. Christoph Boes

All rights reserved

Cover Image copyright © Pedro Antonio Salaverría Calahorra
Dreamstime.com (Image ID: 13534535)
http://www.dreamstime.com/pedro2009_info

All other Images copyright © 2015 Dr. Christoph Boes

Self-published 2016

ISBN-13: 978-0995706064

Table of Contents

Section 7 – The Chemical Industry 7
- Rates 7
- Rate Constant k & Rate Determining Step 9
- Concentration-Time Graphs & Half-Life 11
- Rate-Concentration Graphs 13
- Iodine Clock 15
- Arrhenius Equation 17
- Equilibrium 19
- Nitrogen Chemistry 21

Section 8 – Polymers and Life 23
- Condensation Polymers 23
- Amino Acids & Proteins 25
- DNA 27
- Pharmacophores 29
- Optical Isomers 31
- Carboxylic Acids & Anhydrides 33
- Esters 35
- Acyl Chlorides 37
- NMR Spectroscopy: H-NMR & Carbon 13-NMR 39
- How to predict NMR Spectrum from Structural Formula 41
- Thin Layer Chromatography & Mass Spectroscopy 43

Section 9 - Oceans 45
- Enthalpy Change of Solution 45
- Entropy 47
- Lattice Enthalpy & Solubility Product 49
- Strong Acids and Bases 51
- Weak Acids 53
- Buffers 55
- Buffer Example Calculations 57

Section 10 – Developing Metals 59

Electrode Potentials 59

Redox Equations 61

Rusting & Redox Titrations 63

Example Calculation – Redox Titration 65

Transition Elements 67

Complexes 69

Structures of Important Metal Complexes 71

Colorimeter & Visible Spectrophotometer 73

Section 11 – Colour by Design 75

Benzene & Arenes 75

Reactions of Arenes 77

Aldehydes & Ketones 79

Amines 81

Preparation of Amines & Amides 83

Preparation and Purification of Organic Compounds 85

Dyes 87

Azo Dyes 89

Fats and Oils & Tests for Functional Groups 91

Gas Liquid Chromatography 93

Tips for Organic Synthesis & Combined Techniques Questions 95

Appendix: Periodic Table of Elements 97

How to use these notes

Revision notes (revision cards) are an effective and successful way to prepare for exams. They contain the necessary exam knowledge in a condensed, easy to memorize form. These notes are designed for the final stage of revision and require a thorough understanding of the topics. If this understanding is lacking then help from a professional tutor and additional study of text books or revision guides is suggested.

These revision notes are organized in chapters according to the new 2015 OCR B Year 2 syllabus. Each chapter contains individual revision cards covering all the necessary topics. Everything in *italic* is optional knowledge, aimed at students who want to excel or want to continue with chemistry at university. **Bold** represents important keywords or key definitions. *'Data sheet'* indicates information which will be provided on the data sheet during the exam and does not need to be memorized. Important information and exam-specific tips are highlighted in yellow.

How to memorize: - The revision cards are introduced by their titles and keywords on a separate page. After reading the title you should try to write down the content of the card without looking at the next page. The keywords give you hints about the content. Write down everything you remember, even if you are not sure. Then check if your answers are correct; if not, rewrite the incorrect ones.

At the beginning, when you are still unfamiliar with the cards, it might help to read them a few times first. If they contain a lot of content, you can cover the revision card with a piece of paper and slowly reveal the header and sub content. While you uncover try to remember what is written in the covered part, e.g. the definition for a term you just uncovered. This uncovering technique is for the early stages, later you should be able to write down the whole content after just reading the header. If this is the case, move to the next card. If not, bookmark the card and memorize it repeatedly. Do at least three to four sessions per week until you know all the cards in one chapter word-perfectly. Then move on to the next section. Generally it is better to do shorter sessions more often than longer sessions less frequently.

An even better option is to ask somebody to check your knowledge by reading the header aloud and comparing your answer to the content. Alternatively, get together in learning groups and support each other. Discuss topics which you don't understand; your friend might know the answers or ask your teacher or tutor. More tips about revision techniques, exam resources and corrections for this book can be found on my website: http://www.alevelchemistryrevision.co.uk

Disclaimer: Due to the changing nature of mark schemes it cannot be guaranteed that answering according to these notes will give you full marks. These notes constitute only one part of a full revision program and work alongside other methods, like practising past papers. They have been created with great care; however, it cannot be guaranteed there are no errors or omissions.

Section 7 – The Chemical Industry

Rate of Reaction

Definition of rate with equation
Rate Equation with four points and a tip
Orders in respect to reactants (three points)
Overall order (two points)

Rate of Reaction (Speed)

Definition: Change of concentration (products or reactants) over time

$$r = \frac{\Delta c}{\Delta t}$$

- r: rate of reaction [**mol dm^{-3} s^{-1}**]
- Δc: change of concentration
- Δt: time interval

-> Rate depends on temperature; surface area; catalyst and **concentration of reactants** (pressure for gases) -> see Year 1 revision card "Rates of Reactions"

$$aA + bB \rightarrow cC + dD$$

Rate equation:

$$\text{rate} = k\,[A]^m\,[B]^n$$

- k: rate constant
- [ ]: concentration
- **m: order with respect to reactant A**
- **n: order with respect to reactant B**

- Rate equation indicates how much the rate of the reaction depends on the concentrations of the reactants
- Can be used to calculate rate of reaction
- Products C, D do not appear in the rate equation because rate does not depend on product concentration, just reactants (collision theory: higher concentration -> collisions more likely)
- Catalyst (H$^+$) can appear in the rate equation (might not appear in reaction equation)
- => **rate equation has nothing to do with an equilibrium equation or the mole equation of the overall chemical reaction**

Orders m, n:
- 0 order in respect to A: rate of reaction does not depend on concentration of [A]: double [A] -> no change in rate of reaction
- 1st order in respect to A: double [A] -> rate doubles
- 2nd order in respect to A: double [A] -> rate quadruples

Overall (total) order of reactions: m+n
- **Order of reaction indicates how many of the reactants are involved in the rate determining step (1st: one reactant, 2nd: two reactants)**
- Order of reactants/reactions is determined empirically (experimentally): Concentration-Time graphs & Rate-Concentration graphs

Rate Constant k
&
Rate Determining Step

Properties of k (two points)

Applications

Units of k

Equation to calculate k

Definition of rate-determining step

Relationship between moles of rate determining step and order

Two rules for rate determining step and reactants

Rate equation from single steps with example

Rate Constant k

- the larger k, the faster the reaction
- **k only temperature dependent**
  -> collision theory (kinetic energy > activation energy)
- applications: industry and enzymes
- units of k change depending on order

Calculate k and its units:

$$k = \frac{rate}{[A]^m[B]^n}$$

Example for unit calculation:

first order reaction: rate = k [A]

$$k = \frac{r}{[A]} = \frac{\cancel{mol\ dm^{-3}}\ s^{-1}}{\cancel{mol\ dm^{-3}}} = s^{-1}$$

Rate-Determining step

Definition: slowest step in a multistep reaction

Mole equation of the rate determining step indicates the order of the reactants in the rate equation and vice versa:

1CH$_3$Cl + 1OH$^-$ -> CH$_3$OH + Cl$^-$ slow (rate determining step)

rate = k[CH$_3$Cl]^1[HO$^-$]^1

Rules:
- If a reactant is in the rate equation, it or a species derived from it, takes part in the rate-determining step.
- If a reactant is not in the rate equation, it or a species derived from it, **does not** take part in the rate-determining step.

The reactant of the rate determining step might not be a reactant of the overall reaction. Then the mole numbers of other steps might be taken into account:

Example:

| Step 1: | 2H$_2$O ⇌ H$_3$O$^+$ + OH$^-$ | fast |
| Step 2: | 1CH$_3$Cl + OH$^-$ -> CH$_3$OH + Cl$^-$ | slow |

CH$_3$Cl + H$_2$O -> CH$_3$OH + HCl   (overall reaction)

Rate equation: rate = k[CH$_3$Cl]^1[H$_2$O]^2

The OH$^-$ needed in the rate determining step is formed from two water molecules in the previous step => second order in respect to H$_2$O

Concentration-Time Graphs
&
Half-Life

Three concentration-time graphs (three points)

(Maths – two points)

Definition of half-life

Half-life constant for...

Graph to determine half-life

Equation to calculate k for 1st order reaction from half-life

Concentration-Time Graphs

- to determine order in respect to reactant A by measuring [A] over time
- keep concentrations of other reactants, e.g. [B], constant by using **excess**
- shape of graph indicates order:

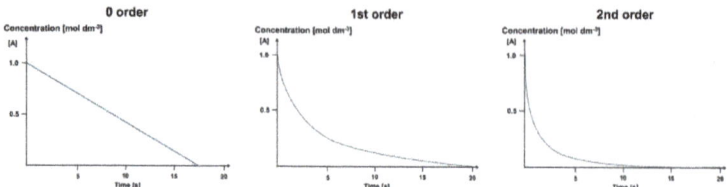

Concentration can be measured with different methods (see Year 1 revision card) -> best if continuously measured (e.g. colorimeter -> absorption proportional to concentration)

Maths
- For first order reactions: graph becomes a straight line if *ln[A]* is plotted against time (slope = -k)
- For second order reactions: graph becomes a straight line if *1/[A]* is plotted against time (slope = k)

Half-Life $t_{1/2}$

Definition: the time required to reach half the initial concentration

Half-life constant for first order reactions:

Concentration-time-graph: 1st order

-> $t_{1/2} = 2.5$ s

Calculate k for 1st order reaction: $k = \dfrac{\ln 2}{t_{1/2}}$

Rate-Concentration Graphs

How to create rate-concentration graphs (two points)
Initial rates method with graph (two points)
Three rate-concentration graphs (three points)
Iodine-clock

Rate-Concentration Graphs

- To determine order with respect to reactant (A) by varying concentration of (A) and calculating initial rate of reactant from concentration-time graphs
- For 0 order reaction: gradient of concentration-time graph equals rate

Initial rates method
- Measure time until set amount of product is formed and calculate rate   *or*
- Draw tangent through concentration at 0 s and calculate gradient to get initial rate for 1st and 2nd order reaction

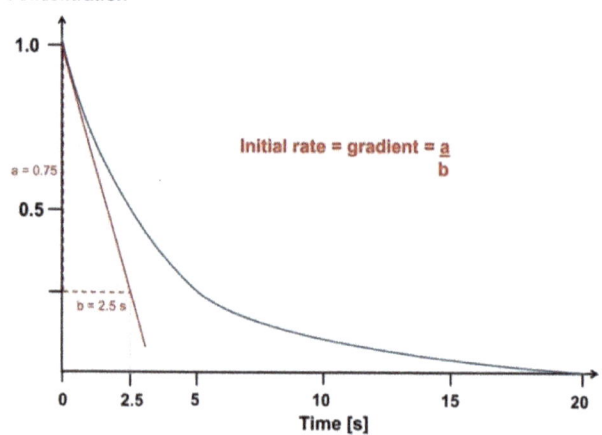

Plot **initial rates against concentration** of [A] to get rate-concentration graphs for A:

Rate-Concentration Graphs

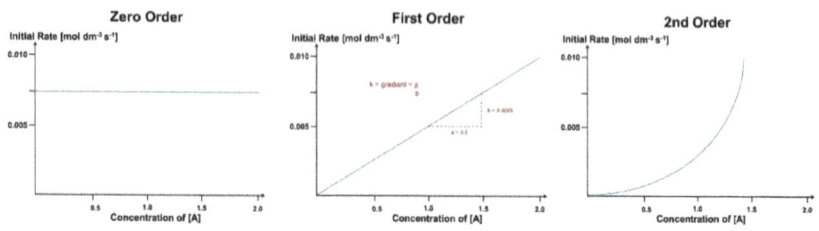

- For first order reactions: k = gradient of line
- If an **enzyme substrate** is in excess then its order changes from 1 to 0 (all active sites are full)
- For second order reactions: the graph becomes a straight line if plotted against $[A]^2$
- Iodine clock: Plot 1/t instead of rate to get same graphs -> much simpler

Iodine Clock

Purpose

Method

Relationship between time and rate (three points)

Two Applications

Iodine clock

-> can be used to determine rate of reaction *(or activation energy E_a)*

Iodine is generated in a redox reaction **(slow reaction):**

$$1)\ 2I^- + S_2O_8^{2-} \rightarrow I_2 + 2SO_4^{2-}$$
(peroxidisulfate)

-> in the presence of starch a **dark blue** complex with I_2 would form,

but is removed immediately (fast reaction):

$$2)\ I_2 + 2S_2O_3^{2-} \rightarrow 2I^- + S_4O_6^{2-}$$
thiosulfate *(tetrathionate)*

-> **colour** does not appear until all of the thiosulfate $S_2O_3^{2-}$ is used up

==The time (t) it takes until colour appears is inversely proportional to the rate (or rate constant k) of reaction==
-> the faster the first reaction the shorter the time
-> this time t is measured with a stop watch and recorded
=> reaction is like a **stop watch** *(therefore called 'clock')*

If we change conditions (concentration/temperature) which increases the rate of the first reaction then the time until the colour appears shortens.

Applications

Rate-Concentration graphs
Plot 1/t instead of rate against concentration
-> measuring the time is much simpler than to determining rate
=> leads to the same graphs

Arrhenius Plot
Plot ln 1/t instead of ln k to determine activation energy E_a
-> measuring the time is much simpler than to determining rate constant k
- see revision card 'Arrhenius Equation'

Arrhenius Equation

Purpose
Arrhenius plot (four points)
Equation for gradient
Equation for E_a

Arrhenius Equation

to calculate activation energy E_a

$$k = A\, e^{-E_a/RT} \quad \text{-> data sheet}$$

- k: rate constant
- A: a constant
- **E_a: activation energy**
- R: gas constant *8.31 J K^{-1} mol^{-1}* ($N_A * k_B$) -> data sheet
- T: temperature in K

Arrhenius Plot
- vary temperature T and measure k (or t -> see "Iodine Clock")
- record in a table and plot ln k (or ln 1/t) against 1/T
- determine gradient **m** of line: **m = - E_a/R**
- rearrange equation towards **E_a = -(m x R)**

$$\ln k = -\frac{E_a}{R}\cdot\frac{1}{T} + \ln A \quad \text{-> logarithmic form of equation}$$

$$y = m * x + c \quad \text{-> general equation for a linear graph}$$

plot ln k against 1/T to determine E_a -> **straight line (descending)**

gradient -m = $\frac{-E_a}{R}$ -> negative gradient (-m)

=> E_a = -(-m x 8.31)

-> **E_a is always positive** [KJ mol^{-1}]

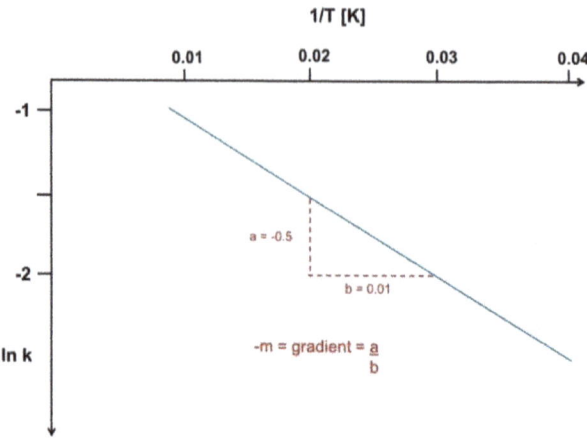

-> see also revision card 'Iodine Clock'

Equilibrium

Properties of equilibrium constant k (four points)
How to approach an equilibrium question (two points)
Example calculation

Equilibrium

-> see Year 1 revision card

Equilibrium constant K_c
- K_c only temperature dependent
- When temperature is increased then K_c increases for endothermic reactions and decreases for exothermic reactions
- If concentration of [C] or [D] is increased *(numerator)*, concentration of [A] and [B] must also increase *(denominator)* to keep K_c constant (equilibrium moves to the left)
- Solids (and liquids) do not appear in the equilibrium equation of heterogeneous equilibria

Equilibrium Concentration Calculation

-> highlight all data given **(bold)** in the question and write down **mole ratios**
-> create a table as specified below

0.90 moles of Nitrogen dioxide were thermally decomposed at 450 C in a container of **23 dm³**. **0.40 moles** of Oxygen were found in the equilibrium mixture. Calculate K_c for this reaction.

$$2NO_2 \rightleftharpoons 2NO + O_2$$

	NO_2	NO	O_2
Initial moles n_i	0.9		
Equilibrium moles	0.1 (n_r)	0.8 (x)	0.4 (x')
Equilibrium conc. [mol dm⁻³]	0.0043	0.035	0.017

Calculate equilibrium moles:
0.4 moles O_2 -> x'
2:1 ratio between NO and O_2 => 2 x 0.4 moles = 0.8 moles NO in equilibrium
1:1 (2:2) ratio between NO_2 and NO -> 0.8 moles NO_2 have reacted -> x
x: reacted moles of reactant (NO_2) (related to x' by mole-ratios)
Equilibrium moles of reactant (NO_2): $n_r = n_i - x$
n_r = **0.9 mole** – 0.8 mole = 0.1 moles => 0.1 moles NO_2 left in equilibrium

Equilibrium Concentrations:

$$c = \frac{n}{V}$$

Divide all equilibrium moles by volume, e.g.

$[NO_2] = \frac{0.1 \text{ mol}}{23 \text{ dm}^3} = 0.0043$ mol dm⁻³

$K_c = \frac{[NO]^2 \times [O_2]}{[NO_2]^2} = \frac{(0.035)^2 \times 0.017 \text{ mol dm}^{-3}}{(0.0043)^2} = 1.1$ mol dm⁻³

Nitrogen Chemistry

Reactivity of nitrogen
Properties of ammonia (three points)
Structures of ammonia & ammonium
Three nitrogen oxides with properties and equations
Tests for ammonium, ammonia & nitrate
Nitrogen cycle (five equations)

Nitrogen Chemistry

Nitrogen
- very unreactive due to triple bond: :N≡N:

Ammonia

Lone pair of electrons on N-atom:
- forms **hydrogen bonds** -> very soluble in H_2O
- forms dative covalent bonds -> **ligands** in complexes
- accepts protons: **base** => $NH_3 + H^+$ -> NH_4^+ (ammonium)

For **structures** of NH_3 (trigonal pyramidal) and NH_4^+ (tetrahedral) see Year 1 revision card 'Shapes of Molecules'

Nitrogen Oxides

NO	nitrogen monoxide, nitrogen(II) oxide $N_2 + O_2$ -> $2NO$	colourless gas
N_2O	dinitrogen monoxide, nitrogen(I) oxide $2N_2 + O_2$ -> $2N_2O$	colourless, sweet smelling 'laughing gas'
NO_2	nitrogen dioxide, nitrogen(IV) oxide $N_2 + 2O_2$ -> $2NO_2$	toxic, **brown**, sharp smelling gas

Tests

Ammonium and Ammonia
see Year 1 revision card 'Test for Ions'

Nitrate(V)
Warm solution with sodium hydroxide and aluminium or Devarda's alloy
$3NO_3^-{}_{(aq)} + 5OH^-{}_{(aq)} + 8Al_{(s)} + 18H_2O_{(l)}$ -> $8[Al(OH)_4]^-{}_{(aq)} + 3NH_{3(g)}$
-> NH_3 turns damp red litmus paper blue

Nitrogen Cycle in the soil and the atmosphere

-> Plants need Nitrogen for growth

1) $N_2 + 3H_2$ -> $2NH_3$ Ammonia (-3)
2) $NH_3 + H^+$ -> NH_4^+ Ammonium (-3)
3) $NH_4^+ + O_2$ -> $NO_2^- + 4H^+ + 2e^-$ Nitrate(III) ion (+3)
4) $NO_2^- + H_2O$ -> $NO_3^- + 2H^+ + 2e^-$ Nitrate(V) ion (+5)
5) $2NO_3^- + 12H^+ + 10e^-$ -> $N_2 + 6H_2O$ Nitrogen (0)

Dr. C. Boes   alevelchemistryrevision.co.uk

Section 8 – Polymers and Life

Condensation Polymers

Condensation polymerization (two points)
Polyamide preparation with two equations
Circling method
Nylon 6,6
Polyester preparation with two equations
Definition of Diol
Drawing lines method
Both functional groups on same molecule
Characteristics of condensation polymers
How to recognise an addition polymer

Condensation Polymers

Condensation polymerization
- Monomers form a polymer and another small molecule (H_2O)
- Monomers must have two functional groups

Polyamide

dicarboxylic acid + diamine -> poly-amide + water

Propane-1,3-dicarboxylic acid + 1,2 diamino-ethane

=> Circle atoms which form the water. The leftover half-bonds form the amide bonds

Nylon 6,6 - called 6,6 because 6 Carbons in both monomers
Hexane-1,6-dicarboxylic acid *(acidadipic acid)* + hexamethylene diamine
$HOOC-(CH_2)_4-COOH$ + $H_2N-(CH_2)_6-NH_2$ -> nylon + H_2O

Polyester

dicarboxylic (dioic) acid + diol -> poly-ester + water

Propane-1,3-dioic acid + ethan-1,2-diol

Diol: compound with two alcohol (-OH) groups

To determine monomers from a chain: draw lines through the middle of the ester bonds and add water (OH, H) to CO and O respectively (hydrolysis)

Carboxylic acid and alcohol group on same molecule -> poly-ester + water

Polyester and Polyamides are biodegradable: can be broken down by hydrolysis due to polar bonds (surgical stitches, which dissolve after time)

Addition polymer: chain is not connected by amide/ester groups, but C-C bonds (non-polar -> no hydrolysis) -> see Year 1 revision card

Amino Acids & Proteins

Definition of amino acids

Optical isomers

Definition of amphoteric

Draw structural formulae at three different pH

Definition of zwitterion

Definition of isoelectric point

Building blocks of...

Protein structures and intermolecular forces

Definition of enzymes

Properties of enzymes

Active sites and inhibitors

Peptide formation with equation and reaction type

Circling method

Two methods of peptide hydrolysis with equations

Amino acids

Def.: alpha-amino-carboxylic acids (NH$_2$ and COOH attached to same Carbon *)

Optical isomers: chiral centre * -> 4 different groups at alpha C (except glycine)

Amphoteric: react as acid & base *(bifunctional molecule)* -> weak buffer

acidic (*protonated*)   intermediate pH (**zwitterion**)   alkaline (*deprotonated*)

Zwitterion: has positive and negative charges at intermediate pH
-> ionic bonds, high melting points (stronger than H-bonds) => solid salts

Isoelectric point: intermediate pH at which amino acid has the same number of negative & positive charges (no overall charge)

Building blocks of Proteins (Polypeptides)
Primary (sequence), secondary (β-sheets, helix) and tertiary (3D) structures
Intermolecular forces: salt bridges – polar interaction, van der Waals.
Hydrogen bonds & covalent bonds (disulfide) -> 3D (denatured by heat & pH)

Enzymes: biological catalysts (proteins)
- They only work well at optimum pH and temperature
- **Active sites:** bind substrates and are stereospecific -> drug target
- **Inhibitor:** molecule which blocks active site (shape similar to substrate)

Peptide Formation (Dimer)

Alanine   Glycine   Dipeptide (AlaGly) (Amide)   +   water
-> condensation

=> circle atoms which form the water, then connect the leftover half-bonds to form a peptide bond

Peptide Hydrolysis

with acid: 6 M HCl, reflux heat; then neutralize
Peptide + H$_2$O (H$^+$) => protonated amino acids (+)

with alkaline: NaOH$_{conc}$
Peptide + OH$^-$ => deprotonated amino acids (-) (carboxylate-salt)

DNA

DNA stands for...
Building blocks of DNA
Formation of the polymer
Formation of the double helix
Base pair combinations

DNA self-replication (five points)

Protein Synthesis:
Coding
Transcription
Translation (four points)

Cis-platin (four points)

DNA

- **D**eoxyribo**N**ucleic **A**cid
- DNA consists of **nucleotides** made up from sugar, phosphate and four different bases: adenine (A), thymine (T), cytosine (C), and guanine (G)
  -> *data sheet*
- The sugar is the pentose: **2-deoxyribose** -> *data sheet*
- The nucleotides (monomers) form a covalently bound **condensation polymer** (phosphodiester). The N-H group from the base and the OH-group from the sugar condense to H_2O.
  -> single strand of DNA
- Two complementary strands are combined to a double helix
- The two strands are hold together by hydrogen bonds between **complementary base pairs**:
  A-T two hydrogen bonds
  C-G three hydrogen bonds

Self-Replication

- DNA needs to replicate itself for cell division
- The double helix splits into two single strands by breaking the H-bonds
- Free floating nucleotides bind do their **complimentary bases (Pairing)**
- The enzyme **DNA polymerase** connects these nucleotides to a new chain in a condensation reaction
- This results in two identical molecules of double-stranded DNA

Protein Synthesis

- Three base codons code for one amino acid (e.g. GCT -> Alanine)
  -> *data sheet*
- Sequence of bases determines sequence of amino acids in proteins
- **Transcription: DNA -> mRNA (complementary code; ribose, U for T)**
- **Translation: Ribosome** uses mRNA as blueprint for protein synthesis
  -> amino acid sequence determined by mRNA (DNA) base sequence
- **tRNA** brings amino acids to ribosome for protein synthesis (shuttle)
- The **anticodon** of the tRNA binds to the complimentary codon of the mRNA
- The amino acids on the other end of the tRNA are joined together by **peptide bonds** to form a **polypeptide** chain (protein)

Cis-platin

- See revision card 'Structures of Important Metal Complexes'
- Anti-cancer drug which prevents cell division
- Binds to DNA by forming a bond to a nitrogen atom of guanine
  -> Cl^- ions are displaced by N from the guanine (ligand replacement)
- Also binds to healthy DNA, which leads to side effects (hair loss)

Pharmacophores

Definition of Pharmacophores
Definition of molecular recognition
Binding depends on... (three points)
Effects of molecule modifications (two points)

Pharmacophores

Definition: The part of the drug molecule that binds to the receptor site and is responsible for its medical activity

Molecular Recognition: Intermolecular interaction between two or more molecules

Binding depends on

- **Size & Shape** needs to fit into the receptor (enzyme) site
  -> can act as **inhibitor** (blocks active site)
- **Bond formation** ionic interactions between charged acidic/basic groups or intermolecular forces (H-bonds, dipole-dipole)
  -> see revision card 'Amino Acids'
- **Orientation** correct optical isomer or E/Z-isomer

-> Modifying the pharmacophore changes its drug activity

-> Modifying other parts of the molecule changes other characteristics, e.g. solubility

Optical Isomers

Definition of optical isomers
Definition of chiral centre
Tip for chiral centre
Draw two optical isomers
Physical characteristics of optical isomers (one point)
(Definition of racemic mixture with property)
Applications (three points)

Optical Isomers

Definition
Optical Isomers (enantiomers) have a **chiral centre** and are **non-superimposable mirror images**

Chiral centre
- **Definition: Four** different atoms/groups attached to one carbon atom -> **asymmetric carbon (*)**
- Look at the entire group not just the first Carbon atom of the sidechain to decide if they are different
- Each chiral centre doubles the number of possible optical isomers of a molecule

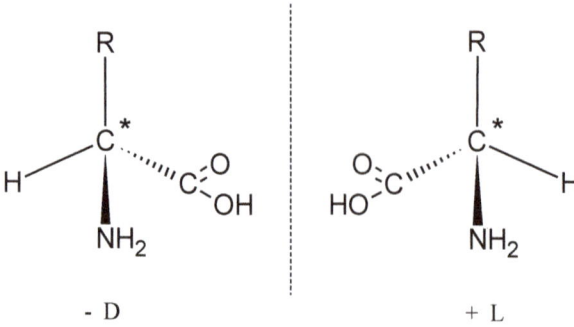

- D   + L

Physical characteristics
- they rotate polarised light anticlockwise (–) or clockwise (+)
  => **optically active**

Racemic mixture (racemate)
- 50 : 50 mixture of both isomers (cancel each other out)
  => **not optically active**

Applications
- important for pharmaceutical drugs (thalidomide)
- amino acids
- enzymes: active sides and substrates

Carboxylic Acids
&
Anhydrides

Naming of homologous series

Name and properties and of the functional group

Characteristics of carboxylic acids (five points)

Acid-base reaction with equation

Three tests for carboxylic acids

Preparation

Organic reaction

Equation for reaction of anhydrides with alcohols (three points)

Carboxylic Acids

Homologous Series: Methanoic acid, ethanoic acid, propanoic acid,...

$$R-C(=O)-OH$$

Carboxyl group: strong dipole -> more polar than alcohols or aldehydes/ketones => OH good leaving group: **nucleophilic addition-elimination reactions**

Characteristics

- high boiling points (H-bonds)
- boiling points increase with chain length (London forces)
- solubility decreases with chain length *(more hydrophobic)*
- IR: show a broad absorption band of OH group at *2500- 3000 cm^{-1}*
- **they are weak Acids**:

Acid-base reaction

2CH$_3$COOH + CuO (base) -> (CH$_3$COO)$_2$Cu (salt – copper ethan**oate**) + H$_2$O

Tests

- pH-Indicator — colour change
- R-COOH + **carbonate** -> salt + water + $CO_{2(g)}$ — **fizzing, carbonate disappears**
- R-COOH + **metal** -> salt (carboxylate) + $H_{2(g)}$ — **fizzing, metal disappears**

Preparation

- Oxidation of primary alcohols or aldehydes

Organic Reaction

- They form **Esters** with alcohols (see revision card 'Esters')

Acid anhydrides

ethanoic anhydride + alcohol -> ester + ethanoic acid

- no catalyst required (more reactive)
- they are hidden carboxylic acids (add water -> carboxylic acid)
- formed by a condensation reaction and split apart in a hydrolysis reaction

Esters

Esterification reaction equation

Naming of esters

Conditions, properties and types of reaction (four points)

Esterification with acid anhydride

Physical characteristics of esters (five points)

Applications (three points)

IR

Two methods of ester hydrolysis

Fats/oils

Esters

Esterification

$$H_3C-C(=O)-OH + HO-CH_3 \underset{}{\overset{H_2SO_4 \text{ conc}}{\rightleftharpoons}} H_3C-C(=O)-O-CH_3 + H_2O$$

carboxylic acid + alcohol ⇌ Ester + water
ethanoic acid + methanol   methylethanoate

- **Conditions:** Reflux, catalyst: concentrated sulfuric acid
- Reversible reaction, equilibrium (low yield), distil off ester
- **Condensation, Nucleophilic Addition-Elimination reaction**
- *Substitution of H of carboxylic acid with -R from alcohol*

Acid anhydride

acid anhydride + alcohol => ester + carboxylic acid
-> No catalyst required (more reactive) => see previous revision card

Physical characteristics of esters
- Nice smell
- Neutral (no acid reactions)
- Low boiling point (no hydrogen bonds)
- Functional group isomers of carboxylic acids
- Less polar than carboxylic acids

Applications
- perfumes & flavouring *(peach, pineapple, raspberry)*
- biodiesel
- solvents

IR

Esters do not show the broad absorption band of carboxylic acids at *2500 – 3000 cm^{-1}* (OH-group)

Ester hydrolysis

hot diluted H_2SO_4: $CH_3COOCH_3 + H_2O$ ⇌ $CH_3COOH + CH_3OH$
                                                    carboxylic acid

hot aqueous NaOH: $CH_3COOCH_3 + NaOH$ -> $CH_3COONa + CH_3OH$
                                              sodium carboxylate (ethanoate)

Fats/Oils

Natural esters of propane-1,2,3-triol (glycerol) with fatty acids
-> see revision card 'Fats and Oils'

Acyl Chlorides

Characteristics of functional group (three points)
Four acylation reactions with equations
Numbering of carbon atoms
Test for acyl chlorides

Acylchlorides

$$H_3C-C\overset{\overset{O\ \delta-}{\parallel}}{\underset{Cl\ \delta-}{\diagdown}}\delta+$$

Ethan**oyl chloride**

Acyl-group: highly reactive C (high δ+ charge -> strongly attracts nucleophiles)
=> **nucleophilic addition-elimination reactions**
=> Cl good leaving group; gets substituted

Acylation reactions

RCOCl + H$_2$O -> R-C(=O)OH + HCl   **Carboxylic acid**

R^{1}COCl + CH$_3$OH -> R^1-C(=O)O-R^2 + HCl   **Ester** (R^2: CH$_3$); **white fumes**

RCOCl + NH$_{3conc}$ -> R-C(=O)NH$_2$ + HCl   **Primary Amide**

R^{1}COCl + CH$_3$NH$_2$ -> R^1-C(=O)NH-R^2 + HCl   **Sec. Amide** (R^2: CH$_3$)

-> similar reactions and products for acid anhydrides (safer, less corrosive)

Numbering of Carbon atoms

- Starts with the carbon of the acyl-group => 1
- Similar to numbering in carboxylic acids

Test for Acyl chlorides

- Reaction with alcohol produces white fumes: HCl
- HCl turns litmus paper from blue to red

NMR Spectroscopy: H-NMR
&
Carbon 13-NMR

Method

Y- and x-axis of NMR spectrum

Four characteristics of H-NMR spectrum

Solvent

Converting ppm into %

Three reasons for use of TMS

Two Applications

Carbon 13-NMR (three points)

NMR spectroscopy

Method: Radio waves of a specific frequency (resonance frequency) are absorbed by the nucleus of an atom. This reverses the spin of the nucleus inside a **strong magnetic field**. (Nucleus must have odd number of nucleons)

Proton H-NMR (nuclear magnetic resonance)

NMR spectrum
Absorption (y) of electromagnetic waves against chemical shift δ (x)
-> gives information about number and position of H-atoms in a molecule:

- **Number of peaks**: number of **different H environments (types)**
- **Position of peak**: **functional group** (different shielding)
  Chemical shift δ: resonance frequency of functional group in **ppm** relative to **TMS** (internal standard, **t**etra**m**ethyl**s**ilane $Si(CH_3)_4$)
  ppm: parts per million -> a percentage
- **Number above peak**: number of protons (H) of same type
  -> from **integration ratio / relative peak area / relative intensity / integration trace (use ruler)**
- **Spin-spin coupling**: main peak splits off into smaller peaks **(n+1)**
  -> doublet, triplet, quartet etc.
  -> indicates **number of neighbouring H: n**
  -> H have to be bound to **adjacent** Carbons
  -> only visible in high resolution NMR

Solvent: $CDCl_3$ *(deuterated chloroform)* or **CCl_4** (H free to prevent interference)

Converting ppm into percentage: % = $\dfrac{ppm}{10,000}$

Reasons for use of TMS
- gives just one, strong signal away from others
- non-toxic and inert
- low boiling point -> easy to remove from sample

Applications
MRS/MRI: Magnetic resonance scanning/imaging with low energy electromagnetic waves (radio waves) in medicine
Chemistry: helps to determine the structure of an unknown compound

Carbon 13–NMR

- number of peaks indicates number of different carbon environments
- chemical shift -> chemical environment of carbon => **functional group**
- for arenes look at line of symmetry

How to predict NMR Spectrum from Structural Formula

Five Steps

Example butanone

Two common peaks

How to predict H-NMR spectrum from structural formula

- **Circle** the same types of hydrogens in the structural formula to get the number of peaks
- Count the number of hydrogens inside the circle. This is the number of hydrogens for that peak (peak area) => write number on top of the circle
- Count how many hydrogens are attached to adjacent carbons (n) to get the splitting pattern (n+1 -> doublet, triplet etc.) => write on top of the circle
- Identify the functional group the hydrogens belong to and get chemical shift from the table *(data sheet)* => write below the circle
- Compare this data to actual H-NMR spectra given

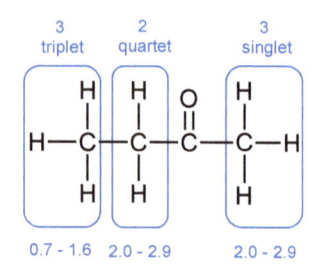

```
    3         2          3
  triplet   quartet    singlet

    H        H    O     H
    |        |    ||    |
H — C —— C —— C —— C — H
    |        |          |
    H        H          H

 0.7 - 1.6  2.0 - 2.9  2.0 - 2.9
```

=> three peaks: 3H triplet   at 1.0 ppm,
                  2H quartet   at 2.5 ppm
                  3H singlet   at 2.3 ppm

Common peaks

A) One peak with peak area 6 (δ = 0.8 – 2.0)   *isopropyl*

Splitting pattern: doublet

B) Two peaks with peak areas 2 and 3 (δ = 0.8 – 2.0)   **ethyl**

Splitting patterns: 2 -> quartet, quintet or sextet; 3 -> triplet

Thin Layer Chromatography
&
Mass Spectroscopy

Purpose of chromatography

Two causes of separation

Application

TLC steps

How to treat colourless compounds

Biochemical application

Equation for R_f value

High resolution mass spectroscopy

Application and Method

Tip

Chromatography

-> Separating and identifying components of a mixture (**solutes**) by degree of interaction with the stationary phase:

- Separation due to different **adsorption** to **solid** matrix -> **TLC, GC**
- or different **solubility (liquid)** -> **GLC**

Application: Quality control in industry (purity & identity)

TLC Thin Layer Chromatography -> see also Year 1 revision card

- See Year 1 revision card 'Chromatography' for method and steps
- Colourless compounds (**amino acids**) have to be treated with **ninhydrin**, **iodine** or **UV light** to make them visible on the dried plate
- Standard method **to separate and identify amino acids** after **hydrolysis** of **proteins**

R_f value:

$$R_f = \frac{a}{x}$$

    a: distance moved by solute (compound) in cm
    x: distance moved by solvent in cm
    R_f: **Retardation Factor (retention factor)**

Mass Spectroscopy

-> see Year1 revision card 'Mass Spectrometry'

High-Resolution Mass Spectrometry

- Accurate Isotopic masses can be used to distinguish between compounds
- M_r of different compounds will vary by decimal places,
  e.g. compound with M_r = 43.9898 is CO_2 not C_3H_8 (44.0624)
  Relative isotopic masses: H = 1.0078, C = 12.0000, O = 15.9949

- **Do not use Relative atomic mass from periodic table for isotopic mass**

Section 9 - Oceans

Enthalpy Change of Solution

Definition of enthalpy change of solution
Equation of enthalpy change of solution
Energetic conditions for a salt to be soluble
Apparatus to measure enthalpy change of solution

Definition of enthalpy change of hydration
Characteristics of hydration enthalpy (three points)
Equation to calculate enthalpy change of hydration
Calculate hydration enthalpies from single ions
Example calculation

Enthalpy change of solution $\Delta H_{solution}$

Definition: Enthalpy change when 1 mole of a substance is completely dissolved under standard conditions

Dissolving consists of two competing processes:
1) hydration of ions releases energy (exothermic -)
2) breaking up the lattice requires energy (endothermic +)

$$\Delta H_{solution} = \Delta H_{hyd} - \Delta H_{latt}$$

The lattice enthalpy ΔH_{latt} (energy released when salt formed) is exothermic (-), therefore sign in front of ΔH_{latt} becomes positive (-- = +)

=> $\Delta H_{solution}$ must be negative ($\Delta H_{hyd} > \Delta H_{latt}$) or slightly positive (due to increased entropy) for a salt to be soluble

=> can be measured with Calorimeter -> see Year 1 revision card 'Calorimeter'

Enthalpy change of hydration ΔH_{hyd}

Definition: Enthalpy change when 1 mole of gaseous ions forms aqueous ions (dissolve) under standard conditions

- increases with **charge density** of ion (smaller ion, higher charge)
- exothermic: electrostatic attraction between ion and dipole water -> **ion-dipole bonds**
- it is a theoretical value (gaseous phase), but can be calculated with the equation below (Hess law), since $\Delta H_{solution}$ can easily be measured:

$$\Delta H_{hyd} = \Delta H_{solution} + \Delta H_{latt}$$

- **add hydration enthalpies of each ion to get hydration enthalpy of the whole salt:**

$$\Delta H_{hyd}(CaCl_2) = \Delta H_{hyd}(Ca^{2+}) + 2 \times \Delta H_{hyd}(Cl^-)$$

=> use also enthalpy cycles/level diagrams to find unknown enthalpy changes

Example Calculation

Calculate if $CaCl_2$ is soluble in water, by using the data below.
$\Delta H_{hyd}(Ca^{2+})$ = -1579 kJ mol^{-1}
$\Delta H_{hyd}(Cl^-)$ = -364 kJ mol^{-1}
$\Delta H_{latt}(CaCl_2)$ = -2255 kJ mol^{-1}

$\Delta H_{solution} = \Delta H_{hyd} - \Delta H_{latt}$
$\Delta H_{solution} = [-1579 + (2 \times -364)] - (-2255)$ | kJ mol^{-1}
$\Delta H_{solution} = $ -52 kJ mol^{-1}

=> $\Delta H_{solution}$ is negative, therefore $CaCl_2$ should be soluble in water

Entropy

Definition

Entropy depends on... (three points)

Equation for ΔS_{sys} with rule

If entropy increases then sign for ΔS is...

Equation for ΔS_{total}

If ΔS_{total} is positive then...

If ΔS_{total} is 0 then...

Tip for answer

Equation for ΔS_{surr}

Tip for unit

Example

Entropy

Definition: Randomness or disorder of a system

Entropy depends on:
  I) Physical State: solid < liquid < gases
  -> increasing freedom of movement & disorder
  => increasing entropy (positive)
  II) Temperature: increasing temperature -> increasing entropy
  III) Number of Moles: Increasing number of moles -> increasing entropy

Entropy change in a chemical reaction

$$\Delta S_{sys} = \Sigma S_{prod} - \Sigma S_{react}$$

ΔS_{sys}: entropy change of the reaction [J K^{-1} mol^{-1}]
S: molar entropies (of products or reactants)

-> **Multiply S by mole numbers from mole-equation**

If the system loses energy by increasing the entropy then the sign for $+\Delta S$ is positive -> contrary to the negative sign for exothermic reactions: $-\Delta H$

-> *Entropy is a form of energy*

Total entropy change of reaction

$$\Delta S_{total} = \Delta S_{sys} + \Delta S_{surr}$$

-> includes entropy of surroundings (ΔS_{surr}) in an open system (energy exchange with surroundings)
-> if ΔS_{total} is positive then the reaction will happen spontaneously
-> if $\Delta S_{total} = 0$ then the reaction is at equilibrium => use to calculate minimum temperature

=> **put + or – sign in front of the entropy value of your answer**

$$\Delta S_{surr} = -\frac{\Delta H_r}{T}$$

T: temperature in Kelvin (0 °C = 273 K)
ΔH_r: enthalpy change of reaction [J mol^{-1}] **(often given in KJ -> convert!)**

-> ΔS_{surr} will be positive for exothermic reactions $-\Delta H_r$: -- => +

Example:

$$2NO_{2(g)} \rightleftharpoons 1N_2O_{4(g)}$$

S (N$_2$O$_4$): 304 J K^{-1} mol^{-1}
S (NO$_2$): 240 J K^{-1} mol^{-1}

$\Delta S_{sys} = 304 - (2 \times 240) = -176$ J K^{-1} mol^{-1}
-> decrease of entropy because of fewer gas moles on product side

Lattice Enthalpy
&
Solubility Product

Definition of lattice enthalpy

Tip

Three characteristics of lattice enthalpy

Solubility product (seven points)

Example Calculation

Assumption

Lattice enthalpy

Definition: Energy given off when **gaseous ions** form **1 mole** of an **ionic solid** (salt) under standard conditions.

-> always negative (ionic bonds are formed)

Characteristics
- to estimate the strength of bonds in an ionic compound (salt)
  -> determines its physical characteristics (solubility, melting point)
- higher charge, smaller ions -> **higher charge density**
  -> stronger electrostatic attraction => increase of lattice enthalpy
- often cannot be measured (very exothermic)

Solubility Product

$$A_aB_{b(s)} \rightleftharpoons aA^{b+}_{(aq)} + bB^{a-}_{(aq)}$$

$$K_{sp} = [A^{b+}_{(aq)}]^a [B^{a-}_{(aq)}]^b$$

- how soluble a salt is, is expressed in K_{sp} (**solubility product constant**)
- the smaller K_{sp} the less soluble
- K_{sp} is temperature depended
- the units of K_{sp} have to be calculated
- determined experimentally (titration until precipitation)
- saturated solution: equilibrium between insoluble precipitate (crystals on bottom) and ions in solution
- important for analytical chemistry and preparing buffers

Example Calculation

The solubility of $Mg(OH)_{2(s)}$ at 25 C is 2.25 g dm^{-3}. What is its solubility product?

$$Mg(OH)_{2(s)} \rightleftharpoons Mg^{2+}_{(aq)} + 2OH^-_{(aq)}$$

$K_{sp} = [Mg^{2+}_{(aq)}] \times [OH^-_{(aq)}]^2$ | solids are not included

Mr = 58.3 g mol^{-1}
Molar solubility S = 2.25 / 58.3 = 0.0386 mol dm^{-3}
[Mg^{2+}] = 0.0386 | 1:1 ratio
[OH$^-$] = 2 x 0.0386 = 0.0772 | 1:2 ratio

$K_{sp} = [Mg^{2+}_{(aq)}] \times [OH^-_{(aq)}]^2$ = 0.0386 mol dm^{-3} x 0.0772^2 mol^2 dm^{-6}

= **2.30 x 10^{-4} mol^3 dm^{-9}**

Assumption: Volume of the solution does not change when dissolving the salt.

-> see Year 1 revision card 'Solubility'

Strong Acids and Bases

pH-Definition

Calculate pH of strong acid

Monoprotic and diprotic acids

Tip

Acid strength depends on...

Conjugated acid-base pairs

Ionic product of water

Equation for calculating pH of strong base

Chemical formula of hydronium ion

pH scale

How to measure pH

Maths

Strong Acids & Bases

pH-Definition:

$$pH = -\log_{10}[H^+]$$

pH of strong acid:

$$pH = -\log_{10}[H^+]$$

=> **[H⁺] equals concentration of the acid** e.g. HCl, unless it is a diprotic acid, like H_2SO_4, which has double the H^+ concentration

Monoprotic (monobasic):   HCl   -> $H^+ + Cl^-$
Diprotic (dibasic): H_2SO_4 -> $2H^+ + SO_4^{2-}$

> -> If the strong acid is neutralised with a strong base, subtract the moles of OH^- from the initial moles of H^+ before calculating the resulting pH

The stronger the ability of an acid to donate protons, the stronger the acid
-> for **reactions of acids** see Year 1 revision card 'Acids'

An acid can become a base if paired with a stronger acid, forming new **conjugated acid-base pairs**:

$$HNO_{3(l)} + H_2SO_{4(l)} \leftrightarrows H_2NO_3^+{}_{(l)} + HSO_4^-{}_{(l)}$$
     base1   acid2   acid1   base2

H_2SO_4/HSO_4^- are a **conjugated acid-base pair (linked by an H^+-transfer)**

Ionic product of water:

$$H_2O \leftrightarrows H^+ + OH^- \quad \text{(slightly dissociated)}$$

$k_w = [H^+] \times [OH^-] = 10^{-14} \, mol^2 \, dm^{-6}$ *at 25 °C*   *(data sheet)*

=> **increases with temperature increase (endothermic bond breaking)**

pH of strong base:

$$pH = 14 + \log[OH^-]$$

=> **[OH⁻] equals concentration of the base** e.g. NaOH, unless it is a dibasic base like $Ca(OH)_2$, which has double the OH^- concentration

H^+ forms H_3O^+ (hydronium ions) with water

pH scale: acidic < 7 neutral < alkaline

pH can be measured with pH-meter or indicator strips

Maths:
    $0.001 = 1 \times 10^{-3}$ -> **use standard form for scientific calculations**
    $\log 1 \times 10^{-3} = -3$
    $\log \sqrt{} = \frac{1}{2}$
    $\log (x \cdot y) = \log x + \log y$

Weak Acids

Equilibrium equation and equilibrium constant equation

How to calculate the pH of a weak acid

Two assumptions

Equation to calculate H^+ concentration of a weak acid

Definition of pK_a

The larger pK_a....

Example calculation

Weak acid

$$HA \rightleftharpoons H^+ + A^-$$

$$K_a = \frac{[H^+][A^-]}{[HA]}$$

K_a: acid dissociation constant [mol dm^{-3}]
-> the larger K_a, the stronger the acid (more dissociation, higher [H$^+$])
[HA]: acid concentration at equilibrium [HA]$_{eq}$

The enthalpy change of neutralisation is less exothermic for weak acid than strong acids, because energy is used up for the acid dissociation

$$K_w = K_a \times K_b \qquad K_b: \text{base dissociation constant}$$

Calculate pH of weak acid:

1st assumption: [A$^-$] = [H$^+$]   (neglects H$_2$O dissociation)
2nd assumption: [HA]$_{eq}$ = [HA]$_{initial}$ (neglects HA dissociation)
-> only valid if dissociation is negligible e.g. K_a is relatively small

Rearrange equilibrium constant equation towards [H$^+$]:

$$[H^+] = \sqrt{(K_a \times [HA])}$$

$$pH = \tfrac{1}{2}(pK_a - \log[HA]) \qquad \text{(-log of the equation above)}$$

pK$_a$

$$pK_a = -\log K_a$$

the larger pK$_a$, the weaker the acid (similar to pH), e.g. chloric(I) acid HClO (pK$_a$ 7.4) weaker acid than ethanoic acid (pK$_a$ 4.8)

Example calculation

Calculate the pH of 0.001 mol dm^{-3} methanoic acid (K_a = 1.6 x 10^{-4} mol dm^{-3})

$$K_a = \frac{[H^+][A^-]}{[HA]}$$

[A$^-$] = [H$^+$]

[HA]$_{eq}$ = [HA]$_{initial}$

[H$^+$]^2 = k_a x [HA]$_{initial}$ = 1.6 x 10^{-4} mol dm^{-3} x 0.001 mol dm^{-3}
       = 1.6 x 10^{-7} mol^2 dm^{-6}

[H$^+$] = $\sqrt{1.6 \times 10^{-7}}$ mol^2 dm^{-6} = 4 x 10^{-4} mol dm^{-3}

pH = -log [H$^+$] = -log 4 x 10^{-4} = **3.4**

Buffers

General definition of buffer

Definition of acidic buffer

Two methods of buffer preparations

Workings of a buffer

pH-Calculation for buffer with two assumptions

Tip

Six applications of buffers

Buffers

Definition: A solution that minimizes pH changes on addition of small amounts of acid or alkali.

A buffer is an aqueous mixture of a weak acid and its salt (conjugate base) in **high concentrations** -> acidic buffer

Preparations

I) Mix a weak acid and its salt ($CH_3COOH + CH_3COONa$)   *or*

II) Mix excess weak acid with a limited amount of strong alkali (NaOH)
  -> salt is formed during the neutralization reaction

Workings of a buffer

$$HA \rightleftharpoons H^+ + A^-$$

Adding H^+: system moves to the left: A^- removes H^+ by forming HA
Adding OH^-: OH^- removes H^+ by forming water, system moves to the right: HA dissociates replacing H^+

Calculate pH:

$$[H^+] = K_a \times \frac{[HA]}{[A^-]}$$

$$pH = pk_a + \log \frac{[A^-]}{[HA]} \qquad \text{Henderson-Hasselbalch equation}$$

[A^-]: concentration of salt (base)   **Assumption:** salt fully dissociated
[HA]: concentration of acid   **Assumption:** $[HA]_{eq} = [HA]_{initial}$

-> If [HA] = [A^-] then pH = pk_a

Applications
- **Blood buffer:** $H_2CO_3 \rightleftharpoons HCO_3^- + H^+$
  pH 7.35 – 7.45 controlled by **carbonic acid-hydrogen carbonate buffer**
  Acidosis: H^+ increases, shift to the left, forming H_2CO_3 -> decomposes into H_2O and CO_2, which is breathed out and blood pH returns to normal.
  Kidneys control HCO_3^- levels
- **Cells:** $H_2PO_4^- \rightleftharpoons HPO_4^{2-} + H^+$
- **Shampoo** (pH 5.5 -> equal to skin pH)
- **Biological washing powder** (correct pH for enzymes)
- **Food:** Citric acid/ sodium citrate, phosphoric acid/phosphate
- *Ocean: $H_2CO_3/CaCO_3$*

For 'Greenhouse Effect' see Year 1 revision card

Buffer Example Calculations

Buffer Example Calculations

I) What is the pH of a buffer, after mixing **100 cm³ 0.10 mol dm⁻³** ethanoic acid with **300 cm³ 0.20 mol dm⁻³** sodium ethanoate?

pk_a (ethanoic acid) = 4.77, K_a = 1.7 x 10⁻⁵ mol dm⁻³

Calculation:

Final volume: 100 cm³ + 300 cm³ = 400 cm³

c (CH_3COOH) = (0.1 dm⁻³ x 0.1 mol dm⁻³) / 0.4 dm³ = **0.025** mol dm⁻³

c (CH_3COONa) = (0.3 dm⁻³ x 0.2 mol dm⁻³) / 0.4 dm³ = **0.150** mol dm⁻³

$$pH = pka + \log \frac{[A^-]}{[HA]}$$

$$pH = 4.77 + \log \frac{0.150}{0.025}$$

$$pH = 5.55$$

II a) What is the pH of a buffer, after mixing propanoic acid and propanoate ions with final **concentrations of 1.00 mol dm⁻³** for both?

b) What is the pH after **6.90 g** of **Na** have been added to 1.00 dm³ of this buffer?

K_a (propanoic acid) = 1.35 x 10⁻⁵ mol dm⁻³

a) pH = pka = -log 1.35 x 10⁻⁵

pH = **4.87**

b)   Na + CH_3CH_2COOH -> CH_3CH_2COONa + ½H_2

n(Na) = 6.9 g / 23 g mol⁻¹ = **0.30 mol**

Mole ratios: Na : HA : A⁻   1 : 1 : 1

In 1 dm³:

n(CH_3CH_2COOH) = 1.00 mol − (0.30 mol) = **0.7 mol**   (-HA removed)

n($CH_3CH_2COO^-$) = 1.00 mol + (0.30 mol) = **1.3 mol**   (+A⁻ produced)

$$pH = pka + \log \frac{[A^-]}{[HA]} = 4.87 + \log \frac{1.3}{0.7}$$

pH = 4.87 + 0.269

pH = **5.14**

Section 10 – Developing Metals

Electrode Potentials

Definition of standard electrode potential

Standard hydrogen half-cell with conditions (five points)

Diagram of electrochemical cell with hydrogen half-cell

Five rules for electrode potential

Equation for calculating E_{cell}

E_{cell} always...

Electrode Potentials

Standard electrode potential $E^\ominus$

Definition: Voltage of a half-cell measured against a standard hydrogen half-cell, under standard conditions

Standard hydrogen half-cell: <mark>1M HCl, 298K, 100 kPa H_2</mark> ($Pt|H_2|H^+||$ ...)
- the voltage ($E^\ominus$) of the standard hydrogen half-cell is **defined as 0V**
- other half-cell contains **1 M ion solution** and is connected by salt bridge
- when two ions form a half-cell (Fe^{2+}/Fe^{3+}) **platinum** is used as an **electrode**
- electrode potentials express the tendency to lose or gain electrons
- ions move through **salt bridge** to complete circuit (maintain charge balance)

Standard hydrogen half-cell ($H_2|H^+$)

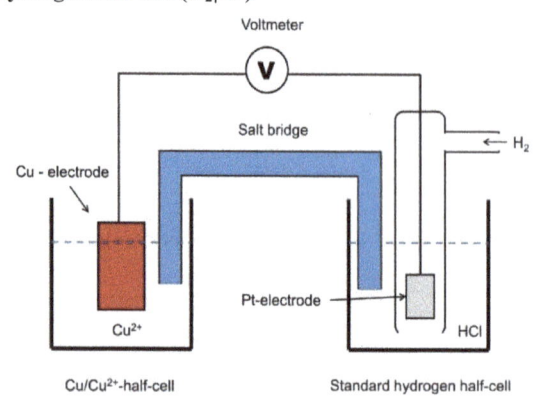

[Diagram: Voltmeter connecting Cu-electrode in Cu^{2+} solution (Cu/Cu^{2+}-half-cell) to Pt-electrode in HCl with H_2 gas (Standard hydrogen half-cell), linked by a salt bridge]

Rules for electrode potential

1) **The greater the tendency of a metal to lose electrons (being oxidized) the more negative the potential (more reactive)**
2) Half-equations are always written as equilibrium with double arrows *(sometimes single arrows in exams/literature due to typeset limitations)*
3) By convention, half reactions of electrochemical cells are always written as a reduction process (species with more positive oxidation number first).
   $Cu^{2+} + 2e^- \rightleftharpoons Cu$
   <mark>(This does not apply to half equations of normal Redox equations)</mark>
4) Potential depends on temperature and concentration (or pressure for gases)
5) **A change of concentration or pressure (gases) which increases the number of electrons (e^-), makes the potential more negative**

Calculating voltage of electrochemical cell E_{cell} (Electromotive force: EMF)

$$E_{cell} = E_{higher\ (Red)} - E_{lower\ (Ox)}$$

-> always positive

Redox Equations

How to combine half-equations (six points)

Predicting redox reactions – circling method (three points)

Example

Prediction can be wrong (two points)

... ions to produce full (ionic) equations
... equations in the correct direction (oxidation/reduction $^\ominus$)
... states to determine the number of transferred electrons

- ... **lectrons transferred must be the same for the full equation**
- multiply both half-equations to get the lowest common multiple (here: 6)
- **cancel** everything which appears on both sides of the equations, e.g. electrons, H^+, H_2O etc. (here: **electrons**)
- to combine to a full equation, add all remaining reactants ($2Fe^{3+}$, $3Zn$) and products ($2Fe$, $3Zn^{2+}$) together on their respective sides

$$Fe^{3+} + 3e^- \rightarrow Fe \quad | \times 2$$
$$Zn \rightarrow Zn^{2+} + 2e^- \quad | \times 3$$
$$3Zn + 2Fe^{3+} \rightarrow 2Fe + 3Zn^{2+}$$
$$\;_0 \quad\quad _{+3} \quad\quad\; _0 \quad\;\; _{+2}$$

Predicting direction of redox reaction (checking if a redox pair can react)

1) half-equation with **more negative potential** loses electrons (oxidation); **more positive potential** gains electrons (reduction)

2) highlight (**bold arrows**) the direction of the reaction according to potential and circle the **reactants** required *(example below: Zn/Zn^{2+} has lowest potential and reaction goes to the left to lose electrons, hence Ag/Ag^+ goes to the right)*

3) see if the **reactants** are present on the left side of the overall reaction equation to decide if the pair of compounds can react

Example

Does Ag react with Zn^{2+} i.e. would the reaction $Zn^{2+} + 2Ag \rightarrow Zn + 2Ag^+$ happen?

$Zn^{2+} + 2e^- \rightleftharpoons Zn \qquad E^\ominus = -0.76$ V

$Ag^+ + e^- \rightleftharpoons Ag \qquad E^\ominus = +0.80$ V

Answer: No, because according to their potentials only Zn and Ag^+ (circled) could react and they are not the **reactants** in the overall equation.

Prediction can be wrong:
- Non standard conditions: change of temperature or concentration
- Rate of reaction too slow (activation energy too high)

Rusting
&
Redox Titration

Rusting with four equations

Corrosion prevention (three points)

General characteristics of redox titrations (five points)

Two reaction equations

Working through a redox titration question (five points)

Rusting

Ox: $Fe \rightarrow Fe^{2+} + 2e^-$ | x2
Red: $O_2 + 2H_2O + 4e^- \rightarrow 4OH^-$
─────────────────────────────────
$2Fe + O_2 + 2H_2O \rightarrow 2Fe(OH)_2$

Secondary reaction:

$Fe(OH)_2 + O_2 \rightarrow Fe_2O_3 \cdot xH_2O$ (hydrated iron(III) oxide -> **rust**)

Corrosion prevention

- **Alkaline Conditions**: reduction equilibrium shifts to the left
- **Barriers** for O_2/H_2O: Paints, Polymer coating, Oiling/greasing
- **Zinc coating**: sacrificial metal with lower potential -> galvanising

Redox Titration

- Is used to determine the concentration of a substance which can be oxidized or reduced
- Needs a suitable indicator, which is difficult for redox reactions (ideally one of the reactants/products changes colour, e.g. potassium manganate (VII) **purple** -> **pink**/colourless)
- No big jump at the equivalence point as with pH titration
- The endpoint is reached, when the solution in the flask takes on the colour of the solution in the burette (unless an indicator, e.g. starch, is used)
- Often I_2/starch complex (dark blue) is used as an indicator (blue colour disappears or shows up). This might require a second redox reaction

Reactions used in redox titrations

$MnO_4^-{}_{purple} + 8H^+ + 5e^- \rightarrow Mn^{2+}{}_{pink} + 4H_2O$ (only with H_2SO_4 dilute)
$Fe^{2+} \rightarrow Fe^{3+} + e^-$

Working through a Redox titration question

- Circle or highlight all data given in the exam question
- Write the dilution ratios and molar ratios on the side of the mole equations
- Work backwards, starting with calculating the number of moles of standard solution used in the actual redox titration from its concentration and volume
- Use the molar ratios and dilution ratios for step by step backwards calculations, as shown in the example calculation (a-e)
- Strike through the ratios after they have been used in the calculation.

-> **For general redox terms and rules see Year 1 revision cards**

Example Calculation – Redox Titration

Redox Titration - Example Calculation

5.0 g of hydrated copper(II) sulphate, **CuSO$_4$ · XH$_2$O**, was dissolved in **50 cm^3 of water**. Iodide was added in excess and reacted with the Cu^{2+}-ions, forming iodine as described in equation (1). A **5 cm^3 portion** of the solution, with the produced iodine, was taken and titrated with **0.10 M sodium thiosulphate** solution, with starch as the indicator (equation 2). The endpoint was reached when the blue colour disappeared. The volume of thiosulphate solution used was **20 cm^3**, as measured with a burette. How many moles (X) of water of crystallisation does the hydrated copper sulphate contain?

1. Reaction: Forming I$_2$
An excess of I$^-$ solution is used to completely reduce the Cu^{2+} ions, whose concentration we want to determine. The moles of Cu^{2+} ions are directly proportional to the moles of I$_2$ produced in a 2:1 ratio.

(1) $2Cu^{2+} + 4I^- \rightarrow 2CuI + I_2$ (2:1)

2. Reaction: Titration of I$_2$ with thiosulphate standard solution (known concentration)

(2) $2S_2O_3^{2-} + I_2$ (blue) $\rightarrow 2I^-$ (colourless) $+ S_4O_6^{2-}$ (2:1)

From the volume of thiosulphate used, we can calculate the number of moles of I$_2$ and subsequently the number of moles/concentration of Cu^{2+} and water of crystallisation:

Steps

a) Calculate the number of moles of sodium thiosulphate used in the titration

n = cV   = 0.1 mol dm^{-3} 0.02 dm^3 = 0.002 mol

b) Calculate the number of moles of Iodine molecules in the 5 cm^3 portion

2:1 ratio: 0.002 mol / 2 = 0.001 mol

c) Calculate the number of moles of Iodine molecules in the 50 cm^3 original solution

1:10 ratio: 10 x 0.001 mol = 0.01 mol

d) Calculate the number of moles of copper ions in 5.0 g of hydrated CuSO$_4$

2:1 ratio: 2 x 0.01 mol = **0.02 mol**   = moles of anhydrous CuSO$_4$

e) Calculate the moles of water of crystallization (X) in hydrated copper (II) sulphate
-> see Year 1 flashcard 'Water of Crystallisation'

M$_r$ (CuSO$_4$) = 63.5 + 32 + 4x16 = 159.5 g/mol

m = nM = 0.02 mol x 159.5 g mol^{-1} = 3.15 g CuSO$_4$ (anhydrous)

m (H$_2$O) = 5 g – 3.15 g = 1.81 g

n (H$_2$O) = 1.81 g / 18 g mol^{-1} = **0.1 mol**

X = $\frac{0.1 \text{ mol}}{0.02 \text{ mol}}$ = 5

The Chemical formula of the hydrated copper (II) sulphate used in this experiment was **CuSO$_4$ · 5H$_2$O**

Transition Elements

Definition
Two d-block elements which are not transition metals
Order of filling the subshells
Two elements with special electron configurations
Where the colour comes from (three points)
Reasons for colour changes (three points)
Properties of their oxidation states (four points)
Two Applications
Reason for their properties
Tests for transition metals (three equations)
Further reaction with ammonia

Transition Elements

Def.: Transition elements have a partially filled d subshell in at least one ion

General Characteristics

- **Sc, Zn not transition metals**: Sc^{3+} and Zn^{2+} do not behave like transition metals -> these ions have an empty or full d-subshell => **colourless**
- **4s filled first and removed before 3d** (4s lower energy than 3d)
- **Electron configuration** Cr [Ar] $3d^5 4s^1$, Cu [Ar] $3d^{10} 4s^1$
  -> half full and completely full d subshells are more stable => **colourless**
- **Coloured** compounds:
  -> ligands split d-orbital into two energy levels
  -> e⁻ can be excited to a higher level by absorbing light ($\Delta E = h\nu$)
  -> remaining light is reflected and responsible for the colour (complement)
  Colour changes happen due to changes in:
    -> oxidation states
    -> coordination number
    -> ligand
- Variety of **different oxidation states** (since there are only small differences between ionisation enthalpies in subshells; *often +2 because of $4s^2$*),
- Oxidation number is written as **roman numerals**, in brackets in the salt name, e.g. Iron(**II**) sulphate: $FeSO_4$, Iron(**III**) sulphate: $Fe_2(SO_4)_3$
- High oxidation state -> **oxidising agent**
- Low oxidation state -> **reducing agent**
- Good **catalysts** because of their **variable oxidation states** and **weak surface interactions** between reactant and 3d/4s electrons (Fe –> ammonia, V_2O_5 –> sulphuric acid, Ni –> hydrogenation) -> see Y1 revision card 'Catalyst'
- They form **complexes** (see revision card 'Complexes')
- Many of their properties are due to their **unfilled d orbitals**

Test for Transition Metals

Precipitation reactions with NaOH or NH_3-solutions
$Cu^{2+}_{(aq)}$ blue $+ 2OH^-_{(aq)}$ -> $Cu(OH)_{2(s)}$ blue precipitate
$Fe^{2+}_{(aq)}$ pale green $+ 2OH^-_{(aq)}$ -> $Fe(OH)_{2(s)}$ green precipitate
$Fe^{3+}_{(aq)}$ yellow $+ 3OH^-_{(aq)}$ -> $Fe(OH)_{3(s)}$ red-brown/rust prec.
-> simplified equations: use aqua-complexes instead of plain metal ions in exams

$[Fe(H_2O)_6]^{2+}_{(aq)}$ pale green; $[Fe(H_2O)_6]^{3+}$ yellow

Further reaction with NH_3
$Cu(OH)_2(H_2O)_{4(s)} + 4NH_3$ -> $[Cu(NH_3)_4(H_2O)_2]^{2+}_{(aq)} + 2H_2O_{(l)} + 2OH^-_{(aq)}$
blue precipitate   =>   deep blue solution

Complexes

Definition of complex
Definition of ligands
Monodentate etc.
Definition of coordination number
Shapes (four points)
Ligand exchange (three points and three equations)
Chemical formulae of complexes (two points)

Complexes

Terms

Complex: Central metal atom/ion + ligands

Ligands: form **dative covalent bonds to metal ion**

Monodentate, bidentate (Ethanediaote: $C_2O_4^{2-}$), **polydentate** (EDTA): number of dative bonds from **one** ligand

Coordination number (x): number of bonds between metal and ligands

Shapes

- tetrahedral/square planar **(4)**
- octahedral **(6)**

-> small ligands (H_2O, NH_3) are usually 6-coordinate (octahedral)
-> large ligands (Cl^-) usually 4-coordinate (tetrahedral)

Ligand exchange

- product complex is usually more stable than reactant complex
- polydentate more stable than monodentate -> **entropy increases** due to more product molecules
- can lead to changes in coordination number, shape and overall charge, if ligands have different sizes and charges

$[Cu(H_2O)_6]^{2+}_{(aq)}$ blue + $4NH_3$ ⇌ $[Cu(NH_3)_4(H_2O)_2]^{2+}$ **deep-blue** + $4H_2O$

$[Cu(H_2O)_6]^{2+}_{(aq)}$ blue + $4Cl^-$ ⇌ $[CuCl_4]^{2-}$ yellow + $6H_2O$

$[Cr(H_2O)_6]^{3+}_{(aq)}$ green + $6NH_3$ ⇌ $[Cr(NH_3)_6]^{3+}$ violet + $6H_2O$

Chemical Formulae

- square brackets are used for complex-formulae (and concentrations)
- **overall charge of complex** = charge central ion + sum of charges of ligands

Structures of Important Metal Complexes

Two different octahedral complexes with bidentate ligands

Two square planar complexes

Structures of Important Metal Complexes

Octahedral complexes with bidentate ligands

[Ni(C$_2$O$_4$)$_3$]$^{4-}$ *or* [Ni(H$_2$NCH$_2$CH$_2$NH$_2$)$_3$]$^{2+}$
Ethandioate   **Ethan-1,2-diamine "en"**

-> **need to be able to draw structures**

Square planar complexes

[Pt(Cl)$_2$(NH$_3$)$_2$]   square planar

cis-platin   trans-platin

-> **cis-platin anti-cancer drug:** binds to DNA and prevents cell division
-> also binds to healthy DNA, which leads to side effects (hair loss)

Colorimeter
&
Visible Spectrophotometer

Purpose of a colorimeter (two points)
Four steps of a colorimeter measurement
How colour appears (two points)

Purpose of a visible spectrophotometer (two points)
Workings of a spectrophotometer (five points)

Colorimeter

- A colorimeter measures the concentration of a coloured solution, e.g. transition metal complexes
- The absorbance of light is proportional to the concentration of the solution

Steps

- Choose a **filter** with the complementary colour, e.g. yellow filter for blue solution to detect only the absorbed wavelength (yellow).
- **Zero** the colorimeter using a cuvette filled with a blank sample (distilled water/buffer).
- Make a series of measurements with solutions of known concentrations (**standard solutions**) to be able to plot a **calibration curve** (linear). The line of the calibration curve should go through the 0 point. The unknown concentration should lie in between the known ones.
- Measure the **absorbance** of the unknown sample solution and read its concentration on the calibration curve.

Colour

- Visible, white light consists of a range of electromagnetic waves: 400 nm (violet) – 700 nm (red)
- A colour appears when its complementary colour or all other colours are absorbed, e.g. blue appears if yellow is absorbed

Visible Spectrophotometer

- To identify a coloured compound or to determine its concentration
- Colorimeters are special types of Visible Spectrophotometers

Workings

- The white light from a light source is separated into its spectrum by a prism
- This spectrum is passed through the sample and the absorbance is measured
- The result is a visible absorption spectrum with characteristic peaks, which allow the identification of the compound by comparing it with a spectrum library or a reference substance
- **Absorption spectrum:** x-axis: wavelength [nm]; y-axis: absorption
- The absorbance of the strongest peak (complementary colour) can be used to determine the concentration with the help of a calibration curve

Section 11 – Colour by Design

Benzene & Arenes

Characteristics of benzene (three points)
Draw p-orbitals and electron clouds (two drawings)
Evidence for delocalised structure (three points)
Naming
Reaction type of arenes with reason
Draw mechanism
Tip

Benzene

Characteristics
- p-orbitals of π-bonds overlap
- π-electrons delocalised (one electron from each carbon)
  => cannot polarise halogens like alkenes do
- high electron densities (electron clouds) above and below carbon ring

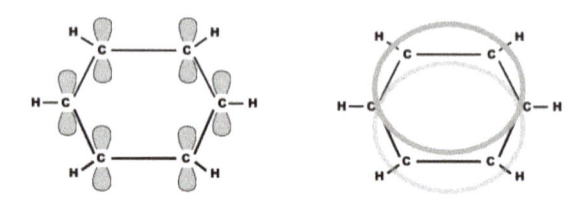

Evidence for delocalised structure
- C-C-bonds have same length (Kekulé: different lengths for single and double bonds)
- does not decolourise bromine water
- hydrogenation enthalpy less exothermic than expected (compared to 3x cyclohexene)

Naming
- 1-chloro-4-methylbenzene (alphabetic, smallest number)
- Name if side group: Phenyl C_6H_5- *(not Benzyl $C_6H_5CH_2$-)*

Arenes – aromatic compounds

Reactions: electrophilic substitutions
-> to keep delocalised system (low energy) *(Alkenes – Addition)*

Mechanism:

Benzene   + E^+ ->   E-benzene   + H^+

E^+: **Electrophile**

-> First curly arrow must touch or cross the inside ring

Reactions of Arenes

Nitration with three equations and conditions (two points)
Halogenation with three equations
Acylation reaction with two equations and conditions
Alkylation with two equations and conditions
Sulfonation with equation and conditions

Reactions of Arenes

-> Electrophilic Substitutions

Nitration with nitric acid

$H_2SO_4 + HNO_3 \rightarrow HSO_4^- + NO_2^+ + H_2O$ **nitronium ion (E⁺)**
$H^+ + HSO_4^- \rightarrow H_2SO_4$ **regeneration of catalyst**

$C_6H_6 \;+\; HNO_3 \;\rightarrow\; C_6H_5NO_2 \;+\; H_2O$
                         nitrobenzene

-> Concentrated HNO_3, sulphuric acid catalyst, below 55° C (mononitration)
-> Reduction of nitrobenzene to aminobenzene for dyes

Halogenations (Chlorination/Bromination)

Halogen carriers: $AlCl_3$ **(**$AlBr_3$**)** or $FeCl_3$ (FeX_3) or **Fe** needed as a catalyst to form **X⁺** ions (polarise halogen)

$AlCl_3 + Cl_2 \rightarrow AlCl_4^-$ (dative) $+ Cl^+$ **(E⁺)**   heterolytic fission; dative bond
$AlCl_4^- + H^+ \rightarrow AlCl_3 + HCl$ **-> regeneration of catalyst**

$C_6H_6 \;+\; Cl_2 \;\rightarrow\; C_6H_5Cl \;+\; HCl$
                   1-**chloro**benzene (phenylchloride)

-> same reaction with Br_2 instead of Cl_2

Acylation (Friedel Crafts) with acylchloride (ethanoyl chloride)

$CH_3COCl + AlCl_3 \rightarrow CH_3CO^+(AlCl_4)^-$ **carbocation**

$C_6H_6 \;+\; RCO^+ \;\rightarrow\; C_6H_5COR \;+\; H^+$
                       phenylketone

-> $AlCl_3$ catalyst, heat under reflux

Alkylation (Friedel Crafts)

$CH_3CH_2Cl + AlCl_3 \rightarrow CH_3CH_2^+(AlCl_4)^-$ **R⁺ (alkyl)**

$C_6H_6 \;+\; CH_3CH_2^+ \;\rightarrow\; C_6H_5CH_2CH_3 \;+\; H^+$ (**ethyl**benzene)
benzene $\;+\;$ R⁺ $\;\rightarrow\;$ benzene-R   (**alkyl**benzene)

-> $AlCl_3$ catalyst, heat under reflux

Sulfonation

H_2SO_{4conc} contains electrophile SO_3

$C_6H_6 \;+\; H_2SO_4 \;\rightarrow\; C_6H_5SO_3H \;+\; H_2O$
                     Benzene**sulfonic acid**

-> heat under reflux

Aldehydes & Ketones

Naming
Properties of Carbonyl group
Preparation of aldehydes and ketones
Mechanism of nucleophilic addition with HCN
Three tests for aldehydes/ketones

Aldehydes/Ketones

Propanone (propan-2-one)   Propanal

Carbonyl group C=O
Permanent Dipole δ+ δ−, but not a good leaving group (double bond)

Preparation: Oxidation of primary or secondary alcohols (see Year 1 rev. card)

Nucleophilic addition with HCN (hydrogen cyanide) to form hydroxynitriles

cyanide (nucleophile, toxic!)   hydroxynitrile (cyanohydrin)
−> CN^- can attack planar carbonyl group from both sides −> **racemate**

Tests to distinguish between Aldehydes and Ketones

Tollens
Test for aldehydes ($AgNO_3$/ammonia, test tube in warm water bath)
$2[Ag(NH_3)_2]^+$ + Aldehyde$_{(+1)}$ −> Carb. acid$_{(+3)}$ + 2**Ag (silver mirror)** + 4NH_3
−> aldehyde is oxidised, silver ions reduced; ketone does not react

Fehling
Test for aldehydes (gentle heating, Cu^{2+}/NaOH)
$2Cu^{2+}$ blue + Aldehyde −> $2Cu^+$ + Carboxylic acid (**Cu_2O** precipitate - **brick red**)
−> aldehyde is oxidised, copper ions reduced; ketone does not react

Acidified potassium dichromate ($K_2Cr_2O_7$)
=> orange to green
−> aldehyde is oxidised to carboxylic acid, dichromate ions reduced
−> ketone does not react
−> see Year 1 revision card 'Alcohols'

Amines

Four types of amines

Property

Naming

Four types of reactions of amines

Mechanism of reaction with haloalkane

Amines

primary R-NH₂, secondary R₂NH, tertiary R₃N, *quaternary R₄N⁺*
ammonium salt

-> 'fishy' smell

Naming
CH₃CH₂NH₂: 1-Ethylamine, 1-aminoethan   -> aliphatic amine
C₆H₅-NH₂: phenylamine (aminobenzene)   -> aromatic amine

Lone pair of electrons on nitrogen causes reactions as:

I) Bases
    CH₃CH₂NH₂ + HCl -> CH₃CH₂NH₃Cl   (CH₃CH₂NH₃⁺ + Cl⁻)
    Ethylamine   ethylammonium chloride (salt)

II) Alkalis (weak): CH₃CH₂NH₂ + H₂O -> CH₃CH₂NH₃⁺ + OH⁻

III) Ligands
    Ligand exchange reaction with [Cu(H₂O)₆]²⁺
    -> see revision card 'Complexes'

IV) Nucleophiles

bromoalkane + **prim amine** -> **sec amine** + alkylammonium bromide
-> **nucleophilic substitution** *(second attack of amine as base)*
-> see also Year 1 revision card 'Haloalkanes'

Preparation of Amines & Amides

Preparation of aliphatic amines with equation and conditions
(Products with excess RX)

Preparation of amides

Test for amines

Naming Amides

Two methods for amide hydrolysis with conditions

Preparation of Amines

Aliphatic Amines from haloalkanes

$$R-X + 2NH_3 \rightarrow R-NH_2 + NH_4X$$

-> **Nucleophilic Substitution**

Conditions: heat in a sealed flask with excess ammonia in ethanol

With excess RX:
continues to substitute H with R until R_4N^+ *(quaternary ammonium) formed*
=> **mixture** *of primary, secondary, tertiary and quaternary amines*
-> *this mixture can be separated by **fractional distillation***

Preparation of Amides

From Acylchlorides

$$RCOCl + NH_3 \rightarrow RCONH_2 + HCl \text{ (NH}_4\text{Cl)} \qquad \text{Primary Amide}$$

-> **Nucleophilic Substitution**
-> See revision card 'Acyl Chlorides'
=> **Test for Amines:** white fumes of **HCl** turn litmus paper from **blue** to **red**

Naming Amides:

$$H_3C-\overset{\overset{O}{\|}}{C}-NH-CH_3$$

N-methylethanamide (secondary amide)

Amide Hydrolysis

Acidic
$CH_3CONHR + HCl + H_2O \rightarrow CH_3COOH + RNH_3Cl$ (primary amide: R = H)
Heat with diluted acid -> carboxylic acid + ammonium salt

Alkaline
$CH_3CONHR + NaOH \rightarrow CH_3COONa + RNH_2$ (primary amide: R=H, ammonia)
Heat with dilute alkali -> carboxylate + amine

See also revision card 'Amino Acids'

Preparation and Purification of Organic Compounds

Apparatus used for preparation
Five purification methods:
Washing (two points)
Drying (one point)
Recrystallisation including method (five points)
Distillation (two points)
Solvent extraction
Tests for purity (three points)

Purification of Organic Compounds

...action mixture safely
...eaters (heating mantel) are used to avoid naked flames which could ignite flammable organic compounds
-> See Year 1 revision card 'Reflux Apparatus' for details

Purification
The products of a reaction are often contaminated with side-products or unreacted reactants. The following methods are applied to remove these:

I) Washing
- A solid product can be washed with water or an organic solvent by filtration under reduced pressure (**Büchner flask**)
- Acids can be removed by reaction with $NaHCO_3$. Water and CO_2 are formed. The water insoluble organic product can be separated by using a **separating funnel** (see Year 1 revision card 'Separating Funnel')

II) Drying
- Traces of water can be removed by adding anhydrous salts ($CaCl_2$, $MgSO_4$)
-> See Year 1 revision card 'Drying with Anhydrous Salts'

III) Recrystallisation
-> Removes small amounts of impurities from a compound, which is very soluble at high temperatures and insoluble at low temperatures
Method
- Hot solvent is added to the impure solid until it just dissolves -> saturated
- The solution is slowly cooled down until crystals of the product are formed
- The impurities remain in the solution, due to their lower concentrations
- The pure product crystals are filtered, washed with cold solvent and dried

IV) Distillation
- The product can be separated from impurities according to their different boiling points
- **Steam distillation:** steam is added to reduce the boiling point of the product, to prevent decomposition at high temperatures
-> See Year 1 revision card 'Distillation Apparatus'

V) Solvent extraction: See Year 1 revision card 'Separating Funnel'

Tests for Purity
- A pure substance has a specific melting and boiling point, which can be compared to literature values (impurities lower melting point)
- **Measuring the melting point:** the solid is slowly heated in a capillary tube, in a beaker of oil containing a thermometer; the temperature is read when the solid melts
- **Measuring the boiling point:** use a distillation apparatus

Dyes

Where colour comes from (two points)
Property of colourfast dyes (two points)
Three types of bonds between dye and fibre
Chromophores (four points)

Dyes

Colour

- comes from reflected/transmitted light (wavelengths); wavelengths of complementary colour *(all other wavelengths)* are absorbed
- absorption causes electronic transition: electrons are excited to higher energy level then later fall back (vibrational energy)

Dyes

- **Colourfast** dyes do not wash out or fade
- They form strong bonds with the fibre:
    - **Covalent bonds** between the dye and amine or alcohol groups from the fibre -> **fibre reactive dyes**
    - **Ionic interactions** between carboxyl (COO^-) and amine (NH_2^+) groups or ionic salt groups ($-SO_3^-$) and amine-links ($-NH^+-$)
    - **Hydrogen bonds** between amine groups (dye) and alcohol groups (cellulose fibre, e.g. cotton) => weakest bond

Chromophores

- Chromophore is the part of the molecule (group) responsible for the colour
- Molecules with alternating (conjugated) double bonds absorb visible light due to **delocalised** electron *(π)* system:
  acid base indicators -> change of electron system by protonation leads to change of colour
- Different functional groups (with lone pairs of electrons) lead to different colours
- Different functional groups also lead to different solubility, e.g. sulfate group increases solubility in water (polar solvent)

Azo Dyes

General formula

Formation of diazonium salt with equations and conditions

Tip

Coupling reaction with equation and conditions (three points)

Two applications

Azo dyes

General formula: R-N=N-R   R: Arene *(Aryl)* – aromatic group

1) Formation of diazonium salt

$C_6H_5NH_2$ + HNO$_2$ + HCl $\xrightarrow{<5\,°C}$ $C_6H_5N_2^+Cl^-$ + 2H$_2$O

phenylamine + nitrous acid   ->   diazoniumion salt + water

Nitrous acid: NaNO$_2$ + HCl -> **HNO$_2$** + NaCl   **(unstable)**

diazoniumion salt unstable -> **explosive**: splits off nitrogen => **< 5 C**

(nucleophilic substitution of N$_2$ by X⁻, CN⁻ etc –> N$_2$ splits off -> aromatic carbocation as intermediate => Sandmeyer reaction)

==Positive charge (+) needs to be on first (internal) N==

2) Coupling reaction to form azo dye

C$_6$H$_5$-N$_2^+$Cl$^-$ + C$_6$H$_5$-OH + NaOH $\xrightarrow{<10\,C}$ C$_6$H$_5$-N=N-C$_6$H$_4$-OH + H$_2$O + NaCl

diazonium cation + arene (phenol)   ->   azo dye

- Diazonium ion **R-N=N⁺** reacts as electrophile **E⁺** (see revision card 'Reactions of Arenes' for mechanism)
- **Coupling: electrophilic substitution** at aromatic compounds (arenes) in presence of **NaOH$_{(aq)}$: base** -> helps H⁺ to leave arene; *cold (< 10 C)*
- **Phenol is a coupling agent:** lone pairs of electrons on oxygen increase the electron density of the benzene ring (positions 2, 4 & 6) and therefore its reactivity

Applications
- Acid base indicators
- Dyes for clothing and fabric

Fats and Oils
&
Tests for Functional Groups

Fatty acids (six points)

Draw structural formulae of triglycerides and glycerol

Triglycerides consist of...

(Applications)

Tests for six functional groups:
alkenes, haloalkanes, aldehydes,
alcohols, carboxylic acids, phenols

Fats and Oils

Fatty acids

- long chain carboxylic acids
- minimum 4C (butanonic acid) -> usually at least 8C (octanoic acid)
- even number of carbon atoms
- aliphatic (non-aromatic), unbranched
- saturated -> no double bonds (animal fat)
- unsaturated contain double bonds (lower melting point, healthier, vegetable oil, fish) -> decolourises **bromine water** (see below)

Triglycerides

$$R^1-C(=O)-O-CH_2$$
$$R^2-C(=O)-O-CH$$
$$R^3-C(=O)-O-CH_2$$

fat

$$HO-CH_2$$
$$HO-CH$$
$$HO-CH_2$$

glycerol

Triglycerides: Triesters of **fatty acids** and **glycerol** (**propane-1,2,3-triol**) -> condensation

Applications
- *Energy reserve and biological membranes (phospholipids, cholesterol)*
- *Manufacture of margarine from unsaturated vegetable oil*

Tests for Functional Groups

Alkenes: decolourisation of **bromine** -> Y1 revision card 'Alkenes'

Haloalkanes: precipitation reaction with silver nitrate -> Y1 revision card

Aldehydes: silver mirror with Tollens' reagent -> Y2 revision card

Alcohols: colour change of acidified $K_2Cr_2O_7$ -> Y1 revision card

Carboxylic acids: fizzing with carbonates -> Y2 revision card

Phenols: **purple** complex with $FeCl_3$; fizzing with alkali metals but not with carbonates -> Year 1 revision card

Gas Liquid Chromatography

Cause of separation

Three parts of the apparatus

Chromatogram with equation (two points)

Definition and application of retention time

Limitations (three points)

GC-MS

Gas Liquid Chromatography GLC

Separation: Due to different solubilities of the compounds in the liquid phase
-> see Year 1 revision card 'Chromatography'

Apparatus
- **Inlet:** injection of liquid (heated to vaporize) or gas sample (not heated)
- **Column:**
  - coiled tube filled with liquid **stationary phase** (high boiling point) on porous matrix
  - stream of unreactive (inert) carrier gas (N_2, He) as **mobile phase**
  - temperature is kept constant
- **Detector**

Chromatogram
- Absorption versus time
- Area under peak gives percentage of individual component in the mixture:

    Percentage in mixture = $\dfrac{\text{area of peak}}{\text{total area of all peaks}}$

Retention time
Definition: The time from injection of the sample to the component leaving the column
-> The component is identified by comparing retention time with that of the pure substance (reference) => if identical then it is confirmed

Limitations
- Unknown compounds might not have reference retention times
- Different components might have the same retention times
- Substances with high boiling points cannot be separated

GC-MS
- An unknown compound leaving GC is identified by its fragmentation pattern in mass spectrometry (MS) -> *airport security*

Tips for Organic Synthesis and Combined Techniques Questions

What to do with the structural formula (five points)
    If the product is given...
    If the reactant is given...

Four tips for combined technique questions

Tips for Organic Synthesis Questions

- Circle and label the functional groups in the structural formula
- To name the compound, identify the main functional group and use this for the name stem
- The main functional group is most likely involved in the synthesis
- Recall the revision cards for each functional group remembering their characteristics, favourite reaction types, reactants, products and conditions
- Deduce from the information given (reactants, products, conditions) what is the most likely reaction to happen. *(If the carbon chain is extended during synthesis CN^- is likely to be a reactant)*
- If the product is given, draw lines through the molecule, especially next to side chains or functional groups, to identify fragments which could give clues to the reactants *(synthons for retrosynthesis)*
- If the reactant is given, go through all possible reactions of the different functional groups from the revision card, and choose the most suitable one according to the product or conditions given.
  Example: 4-aminophenol is the reactant
    - The amino group could react as a base (neutralization) or a nucleophile (nucleophilic substitution, condensation polymerisation)
    - The phenol group could react as an acid (neutralization) or an alcohol (esterification)
    - The phenol ring could act as an arene (electrophilic substitution, *hydrogenation*)
- Memorise diagrams of organic synthetic routes (aliphatic, aromatic, alcohols etc.) from revision guides, to familiarise yourself with the different reaction routes and conditions

Tips for Combined Techniques Questions

- First try to get the molecular formula from the elemental analysis data (-> empirical formula) and the molecular ion peak of the mass spectrum (see Year 1 revision cards)

- Identify functional groups through the information given (test tube reactions mentioned) and IR spectrum (or chemical shifts of H- and C-13 NMR)

- Draw all possible isomers according to the molecular formula and check which structure fits the NMR spectra

- Even if you do not find a structure, describe and characterise all peaks of the spectra according to the data table. This ensures you will still get marks

The Periodic Table of Elements

1	2											3	4	5	6	7	0 (8)
(1)	(2)											(13)	(14)	(15)	(16)	(17)	(18)
					1.0 H hydrogen 1												4.0 He helium 2
6.9 Li lithium 3	9.0 Be beryllium 4		(3)	(4)	(5)	(6)	(7)	(8)	(9)	(10)	(11)	(12)	10.8 B boron 5	12.0 C carbon 6	14.0 N nitrogen 7	16.0 O oxygen 8	19.0 F fluorine 9	20.2 Ne neon 10
23.0 Na sodium 11	24.3 Mg magnesium 12												27.0 Al aluminium 13	28.1 Si silicon 14	31.0 P phosphorus 15	32.1 S sulfur 16	35.5 Cl chlorine 17	39.9 Ar argon 18
39.1 K potassium 19	40.1 Ca calcium 20	45.0 Sc scandium 21	47.9 Ti titanium 22	50.9 V vanadium 23	52.0 Cr chromium 24	54.9 Mn manganese 25	55.8 Fe iron 26	58.9 Co cobalt 27	58.7 Ni nickel 28	63.5 Cu copper 29	65.4 Zn zinc 30	69.7 Ga gallium 31	72.6 Ge germanium 32	74.9 As arsenic 33	79.0 Se selenium 34	79.9 Br bromine 35	83.8 Kr krypton 36
85.5 Rb rubidium 37	87.6 Sr strontium 38	88.9 Y yttrium 39	91.2 Zr zirconium 40	92.9 Nb niobium 41	95.9 Mo molybdenum 42	[98] Tc technetium 43	101.1 Ru ruthenium 44	102.9 Rh rhodium 45	106.4 Pd palladium 46	107.9 Ag silver 47	112.4 Cd cadmium 48	114.8 In indium 49	118.7 Sn tin 50	121.8 Sb antimony 51	127.6 Te tellurium 52	126.9 I iodine 53	131.3 Xe xenon 54
132.9 Cs caesium 55	137.3 Ba barium 56	138.9 La* lanthanum 57	178.5 Hf hafnium 72	180.9 Ta tantalum 73	183.8 W tungsten 74	186.2 Re rhenium 75	190.2 Os osmium 76	192.2 Ir iridium 77	195.1 Pt platinum 78	197.0 Au gold 79	200.6 Hg mercury 80	204.4 Tl thallium 81	207.2 Pb lead 82	209.0 Bi bismuth 83	[209] Po polonium 84	[210] At astatine 85	[222] Rn radon 86
[223] Fr francium 87	[226] Ra radium 88	[227] Ac* actinium 89	[261] Rf rutherfordium 104	[262] Db dubnium 105	[266] Sg seaborgium 106	[264] Bh bohrium 107	[277] Hs hassium 108	[268] Mt meitnerium 109	[271] Ds darmstadtium 110	[272] Rg roentgenium 111							

* Lanthanide series

| 140 Ce cerium 58 | 141 Pr praseodymium 59 | 144 Nd neodymium 60 | [147] Pm promethium 61 | 150 Sm samarium 62 | 152 Eu europium 63 | 157 Gd gadolinium 64 | 159 Tb terbium 65 | 163 Dy dysprosium 66 | 165 Ho holmium 67 | 167 Er erbium 68 | 169 Tm thulium 69 | 173 Yb ytterbium 70 | 175 Lu lutetium 71 |

* Actinide series

| 232 Th thorium 90 | [231] Pa protactinium 91 | 238 U uranium 92 | [237] Np neptunium 93 | [242] Pu plutonium 94 | [243] Am americium 95 | [247] Cm curium 96 | [245] Bk berkelium 97 | [251] Cf californium 98 | [254] Es einsteinium 99 | [253] Fm fermium 100 | [256] Md mendelevium 101 | [254] No nobelium 102 | [257] Lr lawrencium 103 |

Lightning Source UK Ltd.
Milton Keynes UK
UKHW02f1015040918
328262UK00009BA/149/P